WOMEN IN COMBAT

Bringing the Fight to the Front Lines

by Lisa M. Bolt Simons

CAPSTONE PRESS
a capstone imprint

Snap Books are published by Capstone Press,
1710 Roe Crest Drive, North Mankato, Minnesota 56003
www.mycapstone.com

Library of Congress Cataloging-in-Publication Data
Names: Simons, Lisa M. B., 1969- author.
Title: Women in combat : bringing the fight to the front lines / by Lisa M.Bolt Simons.
Description: North Mankato, Minnesota : Capstone Press, [2018] |
Series: Women and war | "Snap Books." | Includes bibliographical references and index. |
Audience: Grades 4–6. | Audience: Ages 8–14. Identifiers: LCCN 2017015341|
ISBN 9781515779346 (library binding) | ISBN 9781515779421 (pbk.) | ISBN 9781515779469 (ebook pdf)
Subjects: LCSH: United States—Armed Forces—Women—Juvenile literature. |
Women soldiers—History—Juvenile literature. | Women in combat—Juvenile literature.
Classification: LCC UB418.W65 S52 2018 | DDC 355.4082/0973—dc23

LC record available at https://lccn.loc.gov/2017015341

Editorial Credits
Megan Atwood, editor; Veronica Scott, designer; Jo Miller, media researcher

Photo Credits:
Alamy: DoD Photo, 24, Heritage Image Partnership Ltd, 26; AP Images, 17, Julie Jacobson, 21; Bridgeman Images:
UIG/Buyenlarge Archive, 9 (bottom), Getty Images: David Turnley, 18, Hulton Archive, 13, The Washington Post, 15;
Library of Congress, 6, 8; Science Source: Colorization by Eric Cohen, 4; Shutterstock: Donald Gargano, 5, Jim Barber,
9 (top), NEstudio, 27 (inset), Peter Hermes Furian, 14, Rainer Lesniewski, 16 (both), 23; U.S. Air Force photo, 20; U.S.
Army photo by Sgt. Kandi Huggins, cover; U.S. Navy photo by Petty Officer 3rd Class M. Jang, 22; Wikimedia: The U.S.
Army, 10, U.S. Department of Defense, 25

Design Elements: Shutterstock: Allexxandar, Eky Studio, udra11

Printed and bound in Canada.
010395F17

TABLE OF CONTENTS

The Revolutionary War (1775 – 1783) was a bloody conflict where colonists and the British clashed. In 1781, Deborah Sampson decided to do something. She started dressing like a male soldier, using the name Robert Shurtliff. Living with that secret was no easy task. She once removed a bullet from her thigh, so that a doctor wouldn't discover her. She was shot again four months later in the shoulder. But it was a fever that forced her to the doctor in 1783. The doctor wrote a letter to a general, telling him Sampson's secret. Instead of punishing Sampson, the general helped her receive an honorable discharge for her service.

Deborah Sampson delivering a letter to General George Washington.

4

"The future of women in the military seems assured. There will be for some time debate about whether and where women can serve in combat...what may be lost in time is the story of how it happened. The barriers of sex and race were, and sometimes still are, very difficult to overcome."

— *Lieutenant Colonel Charity Adams Earley, Women's Army Corps, World War II*

FACT

In 1775 in Groton, Massachusetts, women put on their husbands' clothes and defended the Nashua River Bridge using pitchforks and muskets. The women also captured a Tory, an American who sided with the enemy. He was carrying information in his boots to the British.

Some women fought alongside their husbands, like Tyonajanegen, a member of the Oneida Nation. She was the first American Indian woman to serve in the U.S. military, though she was never officially recognized by them.

Women didn't stop there. Diaries and journals documented combat service by women in the War of 1812. Elizabeth Newcom disguised herself as a man in order to join the Mexican-American War (1846–1848). She became Bill Newcom in 1847.

Women again engaged in battle during the Civil War (1861–1865). Between 400 and 750 women became soldiers. Although it was illegal for women to fight, some did so alongside their husbands and brothers openly. Most of them, however, decided to disguise themselves.

Jennie Hodgers used the name Albert Cashier to fight in 40 battles. Frances Louisa Clayton saw her husband get killed but stepped over his body to continue fighting. Sarah Rosetta Wakeman adopted a man's name to join the 153rd New York Infantry Regiment. Even after she got sick and died, Sarah's secret continued. She is buried as Private Lyons Wakeman.

Frances Louisa Clayton

Staying disguised wasn't difficult. Soldiers were recruited from average citizens without military training. Most soldiers had bathroom privacy. Women tried to avoid being injured, killed, or captured to keep their secret. Six female soldiers serving in the Civil War were discovered, however, when they gave birth.

Medal of Honor

Dr. Mary Edwards Walker graduated from medical school in 1855. When the war began, she applied to work for the U.S. War Department. She treated soldiers while under attack at Bull Run and was a prisoner of war for four months in 1864. She was awarded the Medal of Honor — the highest military award — in 1865 from President Andrew Johnson. She was the first woman ever to be awarded this medal.

In 1917, however, the requirements for eligibility changed: Medal of Honor recipients couldn't be civilians. Dr. Walker was asked to give her medal back, but she refused. Although her recognition was taken away, she wore the actual medal until her death in 1919. President Jimmy Carter returned the recognition to her family in 1977.

"The firing took place about eight o'clock in the morning. There was a heavy cannonading all day and a sharp firing of infantry... I had to face the enemy bullets with my regiment. I was under fire about four hours and laid on the field of battle all night."

— Sarah Rosetta Wakeman, in a letter to her family

Chapter 2

WORLD WARS

During World War I (1914–1918). the United States Navy decided they could "free a man to fight" by enlisting women for noncombat military jobs. About 12,000 women became yeomen (F), the F standing for female. Most jobs were clerical, or in offices, but some yeomen became supervisors or worked at shipyards.

Between August and November of 1918, the Marine Corps enlisted 305 "Marinettes." These women stayed in the United States and were paid the same as the men to do various jobs. Many of these jobs were clerical. However, some Marinettes became naval rail shipment supervisors or radio operators.

When World War I ended in November 1918, 34,000 women had served in the military as typists, electricians, and intelligence staff. Even if they hadn't been in direct combat, some of those women had been near or on enemy lines, just as the men had.

Marinettes

"Hello Girls"

Because they were bilingual in English and French, 223 U.S. telephone operators served overseas. Hired by the U.S. Army Signal Corps, they were called "Hello Girls." They were paid the same as male soldiers with similar responsibilities and served in war zones. When they returned to the United States, however, they were told they hadn't really served in the military. They wouldn't have been protected if captured. They couldn't receive military awards, although seven women had earned Distinguished Service Medals for being dedicated and heroic. They were not even considered veterans. The "Hello Girls" finally earned veteran status in 1979, over 60 years after they'd served.

"Hello Girls" in action

In World War II (1939–1945) there were not enough men for all military roles. Most women didn't serve in combat, at least initially. But many sacrificed their lives working in military positions.

WAAC recruits

In May 1942, the Women's Army Auxiliary Corps (WAAC) was established. Oveta Culp Hobby, a wife and mother who had gone to law school, managed this corps. Women worked important jobs away from the front lines, including operating control towers and loading shells. In July 1943, the organization became the Women's Army Corps (WAC), giving the women military rank.

In July 1942, a bill was approved to establish a women's reserve unit in the U.S. Navy. It created the Women Accepted for Voluntary Emergency Service (WAVES). Under the same bill, the U.S. Marines and the U.S. Coast Guard established the SPARs, or Semper Paratus! Always Ready! Both of these groups provided clerical help initially but grew to offer other positions in aviation, technology, and others.

In July 1943, Jacqueline Cochran and Nancy Love merged their two women's pilot organizations into the Women Airforce Service Pilots (WASP). Just over 1,000 female pilots instructed male pilots, towed targets, and transported planes across the United States.

"Given the serious attacks of German submarines along the Atlantic coast, it is irresponsible to take time to put butterflies in the Navy."

— *Representative Beverly M. Vincent in criticizing the Navy bill to establish a Women's Naval Reserve*

IN WORLD WAR II, MORE THAN:
- 350,000 women served in various military capacities
- 30,000 Army nurses worked in combat zones
- 200 Army nurses lost their lives
- 1,600 nurses won both noncombat and combat awards
- 550 Women's Army Corps (WACs) also received combat honors

Chapter 3

INTEGRATION AND OVERSEAS WARS

On June 2, 1948, Congress passed the Women's Armed Services Integration Act. Women were finally and permanently included in the military branches. However, one rule stated that promotions were restricted. Another rule stated that taking part in any combat — land, sea, or air — wasn't allowed.

When more than 130,000 North Korean soldiers first invaded South Korea in June 1950, only one U.S. military woman was there. U.S. Army Nurse Captain Viola McConnell planned for and evacuated 643 American dependents, including sick children, four pregnant women, and two elderly women.

As the Korean War (1950–1953) continued, 70 percent of the nurses were assigned to Mobile Army Surgical Hospital (MASH) units. Wherever the servicemen traveled for combat, the hospitals moved with them. The military denied requests for anyone other than nurses to go to combat zones. However, some estimates say that at least 74,000 women still served in this war.

In the 1950s, women who joined the military participated in basic training. However, they also had appearance and etiquette classes. For example, the military encouraged women to go to a hairdresser and to carry white gloves. They also suggested that it was impolite for a woman to order her own meal on a date.

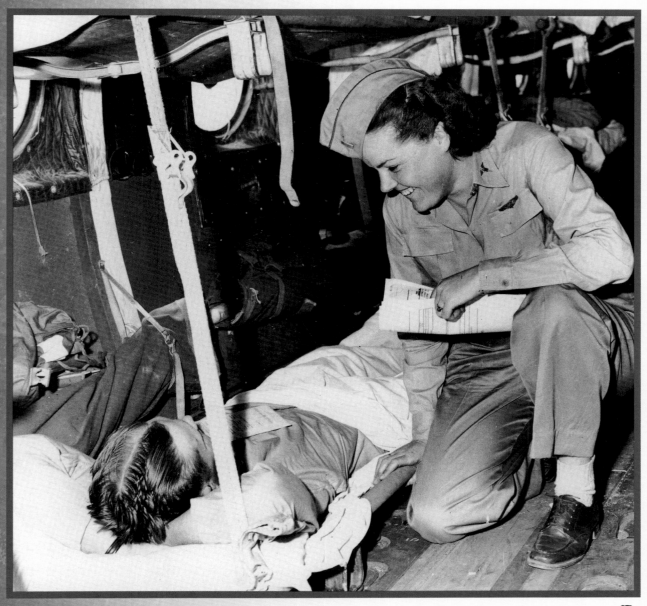

U.S. Air Force flight nurse

The Vietnam War (1954–1975) was similar to the Korean War for women. Although not officially deployed to combat zones, that's exactly where they were. Of the roughly 250,000 women in the U.S. military during this war, 10,000 were stationed in Vietnam. Between 5,000 and 6,000 were nurses in combat zones. The first military nurse killed in Vietnam was hit by an enemy rocket when she was in her quarters.

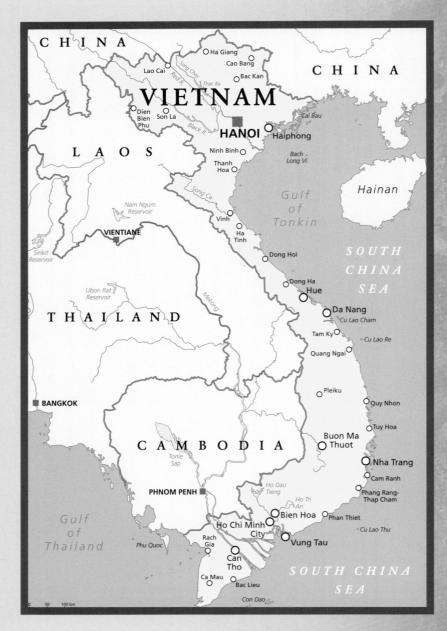

Many firsts happened during this war. Anna Mae Hays and Elizabeth Hoisington became the first female brigadier generals in the Army in 1970. Former first lady Mamie Eisenhower presented her deceased husband's stars to Hays, the same stars President Eisenhower wore upon his promotion. Hazel Johnson was the first African-American general in all the military branches when she was promoted to brigadier general in 1979.

More changes happened after the war. In 1977, women qualified for noncombat airplane duty in the Air Force and were also allowed to work aboard ships in the Coast Guard.

Hazel Johnson

FACT

In 1972, one in every 30 recruits was a woman. Four years later, one in every 13 recruits was female.

In September 1983, the Army closed 23 jobs once open to women, due to possible combat or active fighting situations. However, a month later, Operation Urgent Fury began in Grenada. The country's leader had been assassinated, and more than 1,000 Americans lived in the unstable country. U.S. troops were deployed. Though not officially in combat, 200 Army women earned Imminent Danger Pay (IDP) during this operation.

In a similar situation, Panama declared war on the United States in December 1989. The United States responded with Operation Just Cause, deploying 25,000 troops, including 800 women. Approximately 150 women served in combat zones.

Captain Linda Bray was the first woman to lead a U.S. military operation. The goal was to take over a kennel that housed attack dogs. The simple operation ended up being a three-hour gunfight, but it was a success. Some people, however, believed Bray received too much attention because she was a woman. Due to Bray and other female soldiers receiving a non-combat medal instead of a combat one — along with other reasons — Bray left the Army.

Captain Linda Bray

"If they are going to let us wear the uniform, then they ought to let us defend it. Otherwise, don't let us wear it."

— *Female paratrooper in Panama*

Chapter 4

COMBAT BY AIR AND SEA

The First Gulf War (1990–1991) became a historic time for women. They made up 11 percent of the U.S. military and almost 41,000 were deployed — a record number at the time. Around 40 percent of those women were African-American.

Military women performed various jobs in the United States and around the world. They piloted aircraft, launched missiles, used machine guns, guarded bases, secured harbors, commanded units, and other assignments. According to the military, none of these positions were direct combat positions when ground attacks were started by U.S. forces.

U.S. soldier tending to an Iraqi soldier

In 1948, the Integration Act banned women from flying combat missions. In November 1991, after much debate, Congress passed a law that repealed this act. But it wasn't until April 1993 when the Secretary of Defense ordered all branches to allow women to fly in combat that the ban was truly overturned. In addition, the Navy was asked to allow women on combat ships.

On March 22, 1996, Sergeant Heather Lynn Johnson became the first woman to guard the Tomb of the Unknown Soldier. The tomb is in Washington, D.C., and honors U.S. soldiers from four major wars.

Commanding Officers

When the First Gulf War began in 1990, the Navy asked the Coast Guard for ships and crews to help in the Iraq and Kuwait areas. The Navy requested that the Coast Guard replace the women in leadership roles. But the Coast Guard had already fully integrated with women filling all available positions.

Lieutenant Jane Hartley of the Coast Guard said, "The Navy got its underwear in a bunch because we had ships going over to [Kuwait/Iraq] with women as leaders in the theater and that was a real shakeup for them. They said, 'You can't do that!' And we said, 'Then you can't have the ships because you can't take the [commanding officers] off the vessels.'"

"Amid the international hubbub [around the First Gulf War], American service personnel, regular and reserve, male and female, were quietly doing what soldiers have always done when the call to duty came. They were getting their lives in order, assembling their field gear, saying good-bye to loved ones and friends, and preparing to do what they had been trained to do."

– Major General Jeanne Holm, U.S. Air Force (Retired), in Women in the Military: An Unfinished Revolution

In 1993, female combat pilots took off in the military—literally. As an Air Force Academy cadet, Martha McSally dreamed of being a fighter pilot. Accepted into fighter pilot school in 1993, she attended the next year. When she completed her training, McSally was the first female Air Force combat pilot to fly missions in 1995. She flew 325 combat hours in Afghanistan and Iraq. In 2004, she became the first woman to command a fighter squadron.

Martha McSally

"The plane doesn't know or care about your gender as a pilot, nor do the ground troops who need your support. You just have to perform. That's all anyone cares about when you're up there — that you do your job, and that you do it exceptionally well."

— Lieutenant Colonel Christine Mau, U.S. Air Force, F-35 fighter pilot

FACT

The first female combat pilot in the world was Sabiha Gökçen of Turkey from the late 1930s.

Vernice Armour originally wanted to be a police officer on horseback. In college she saw a picture of an African-American woman in a flight suit and liked that idea. After working as a corrections officer and police officer, Armour went to flight school. She became the first African-American female combat pilot with the Marine Corps. She flew missions in Iraq in 2003, making her the first female African-American combat pilot in the U.S. military.

Vernice Armour

Firsts for Women Pilots

• JEANNIE LEAVITT — first fighter pilot in the Air Force (1992)
first fighter wing commander (2012)

• CAREY LOHRENZ and KARA HULTGREEN — first fighter pilots in the Navy (1994)

• MARTHA MCSALLY — first combat pilot in the Air Force in Iraq (1995)
first fighter squadron commander (2004)

• SARAH DEAL BURROW — first female pilot in the Marine Corps (1995)

• VERNICE ARMOUR — first African-American combat pilot in the U.S. military (2003)

• NICOLE MALACHOWSKI — first military air demonstration team fighter pilot with the U.S. Air Force Thunderbirds (2005)

• SARA JOYNER — first aircraft carrier air wing commander in the Navy (2013)

Besides taking to the sky, women started to command the waves.

Kathleen McGrath became the first woman commander on a U.S. Navy warship that carried guided missiles in the Persian Gulf in 2000. Before she died at age 50, McGrath had earned several awards.

In 2009, the captain of the *Maersk Alabama* was kidnapped by Somali pirates. Michelle Howard was the commander of the task force who rescued him. Five years later, Howard became the first African-American four-star admiral in the Navy, the highest-ranking African-American in the U.S. military.

"I can get shot at; I just can't shoot back."
– *Air Force Lieutenant Colonel Kelly Hamilton*

Michelle Howard

On September 11, 2001, terrorists flew two planes into the World Trade Center. Another hit the Pentagon, while a fourth plane crashed before hitting its target. Nearly 3,000 people were killed. Hundreds of thousands of military personnel — including approximately 280,000 women — were deployed overseas, the largest deployments since the First Gulf War. As of October 2015, more than 1,000 soldiers were wounded and 161 were killed.

Getting Justice

In November 2012, four female war veterans sued the Department of Defense: Marine First Lieutenant Colleen Farrell, Marine Reserves Captain Zoe Bedell, Army Staff Sergeant Jennifer Hunt, and Air Guard Major Mary Jennings Hegar. All of the women had served in Iraq or Afghanistan. Staff Sergeant Hunt and Major Hegar had been given a Purple Heart award for combat.

These four veterans claimed the military's rule against women in ground combat was unfair. Some of the veterans had gone on missions with combat infantrymen. But since these jobs were considered temporary, their combat experience was not officially recognized. They also couldn't apply for other combat positions.

As of January 2017, the case was still being heard in military court.

NO EXCEPTIONS

For the first time in its history, the Ranger School, one of the most difficult in the military, opened to women in 2015. The two-month course prepares soldiers for combat. Captain Kristen Griest and First Lieutenant Shaye Haver were the first two female graduates in August 2015. Haver continued serving as an Apache helicopter pilot. Griest became the first woman infantry officer.

Army Captain Kristen Griest during combatives training

24

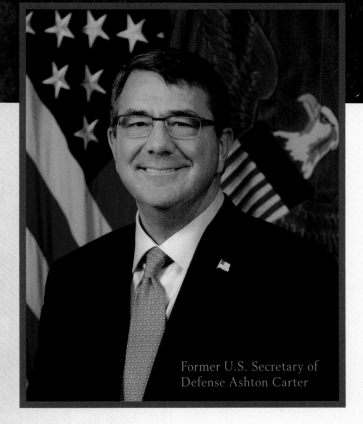

Former U.S. Secretary of Defense Ashton Carter

In December 2015, U.S. Secretary of Defense Ashton Carter sent a memo to all the military departments. He wanted the 1994 Direct Ground Combat Definition and Assignment Rule repealed. This repeal meant integrating women into all branches of the military starting January 1, 2016. This memo states that anyone, "regardless of gender," who can achieve the necessary standards can serve in any military position. This rule included opening 220,000 combat positions to women. Finally, direct ground combat duty was an option for women. There would be no exceptions.

Countries around the world allowed women in combat positions long before the United States did. In World War I (1914–1918), Italian women fought on the north border. During World War II (1939–1945), the Soviets estimate that 800,000 women fought. Approximately 100,000 women in Yugoslavia were guerrilla soldiers between 1941 and 1945. In Israel's War of Independence in 1948, women both fought and led.

Women's military training, Great Patriotic War, Soviet Union, 1941

Women have been active in combat in Canada and Sweden since 1989, Denmark since 1998, and Germany and New Zealand since 2001. The ban on women in combat in Britain ended in 2016.

The military has finally changed its rules. Women are now legally allowed — and finally officially recognized — in all forms of combat, whether at sea, on land, or in the sky.

FACT

Women now make up 15 percent of Department of Defense active-duty military personnel.

"Women who come back to their communities after service are strong, resilient, and come back with leadership and technical skills with lots to give."

— Kayla Williams, a veteran and the director of the Department of Veterans Affairs' Center for Women Veterans

TIMELINE

1775–1783
REVOLUTIONARY WAR
American women put on their husbands' clothes and defend the Nashua River Bridge

1812
WAR OF 1812
Diaries and journals document combat service by women

1861–1865
U.S. CIVIL WAR
Between 400 and 750 women secretly become soldiers

1914–1918
WORLD WAR I
12,000 women become U.S. Navy yeomen

305 women join the U.S. Marine Corps as Marinettes

223 women sign up to join U.S. Army Signal Corps "Hello Girls," or bilingual telephone operators, overseas

34,000 women serve in the military, some near or on enemy lines

1939–1945
WORLD WAR II
1942, Women's Army Auxiliary Corps (WAAC) is established

1942, women join the U.S. Navy Women, Voluntary Emergency Service, or WAVES

1942, women join the U.S. Marine and U.S. Coast Guard, Semper Paratus! Always Ready, or SPARs

1943, Women's Army Corps (WAC) is established, giving women military rank

1943, the Women Airforce Service Pilots, or WASP, is founded

1948
Congress passes the Women's Armed Services Integration Act; however, promotions and combat are not allowed

1950–1953
KOREAN WAR
Approximately 74,000 women serve

1954–1975

VIETNAM WAR

Roughly 250,000 women are in the military with about 10,000 stationed in Vietnam

Between 5,000 and 6,000 nurses serve in combat zones

1979

The U.S. Coast Guard integrates women into all military positions

1983

The Army closes 23 jobs, once open to women, due to possible combat or active fighting situations

During Operation Urgent Fury in Grenada, 200 Army women earn Imminent Danger Pay

1989

During Operation Just Cause, approximately 150 women serve in combat zone

1990–1991

FIRST GULF WAR

Women make up 11 percent of the U.S. military and perform various military jobs around the world

1991

Congress repeals the 1948 act that banned women from flying

1993

The U.S. Secretary of Defense orders all branches to allow women to fly in combat; the Navy is asked to allow women on combat ships

2001

After September 11, 2001, approximately 280,000 women are deployed overseas

2012

Four female war veterans sue the Department of Defense, claiming the military's rule against women in ground combat is unfair

2016

The U.S. Secretary of Defense repeals the 1994 rule that did not allow ground combat in all military branches; 220,000 combat positions are open to women

Glossary

assassinate—to kill someone important or famous by surprise

auxiliary—extra or additional

bilingual—being able to speak two languages

civilians—people who are not in the military

deployment—when troops move to a particular location to prepare for military action

etiquette—the practice of good manners in social situations

gender—male or female

guerrilla—someone who fights in a conflict or war but who is not part of the military

imminent—about to happen

integration—the process of accepting equals into a group

promotion—the moving up in rank or position

quarters—where someone lives

recruited—when new members are added to a group

repealed—cancelled or voided

squadron—a smaller unit or group in the military

veterans—former members of the military

Read More

Coleman, Miriam. *Women in the Military.* Women Groundbreakers. New York: PowerKids Press, 2015.

Gillespie, Katie. *Fighter Jets.* Mighty Military Machines. New York: Let's Read, 2016.

Miller, Nancy. *My Mom Is in the Navy.* Military Families. New York: PowerKids Press, 2016.

Internet Sites

Use FactHound to find Internet sites related to this book.

Here's all you do:
Visit *www.facthound.com*

Just type in 9781515779346 and go.

Critical Thinking Questions

1. In early wars, it was illegal for a U.S. woman to be in combat. Many women who still wanted to fight for their country disguised themselves. Other than the ways already listed, how else do you think women kept their gender secret?

2. What were some frustrations for women who wanted to be in battle but were banned from it? Use the text to find examples.

3. U.S. women were allowed in combat in the air and by sea more than 20 years before women were allowed in direct ground combat. What do you think are some reasons for this?

Index